Joy in looking and comprehending
is nature's most beautiful gift.
—Albert Einstein

To Leonard Lee Rue III,
who was the first to encourage
my wildlife watching by
sharing his knowledge
of animals with me.

SECRETS OF A
WILDLIFE
WATCHER

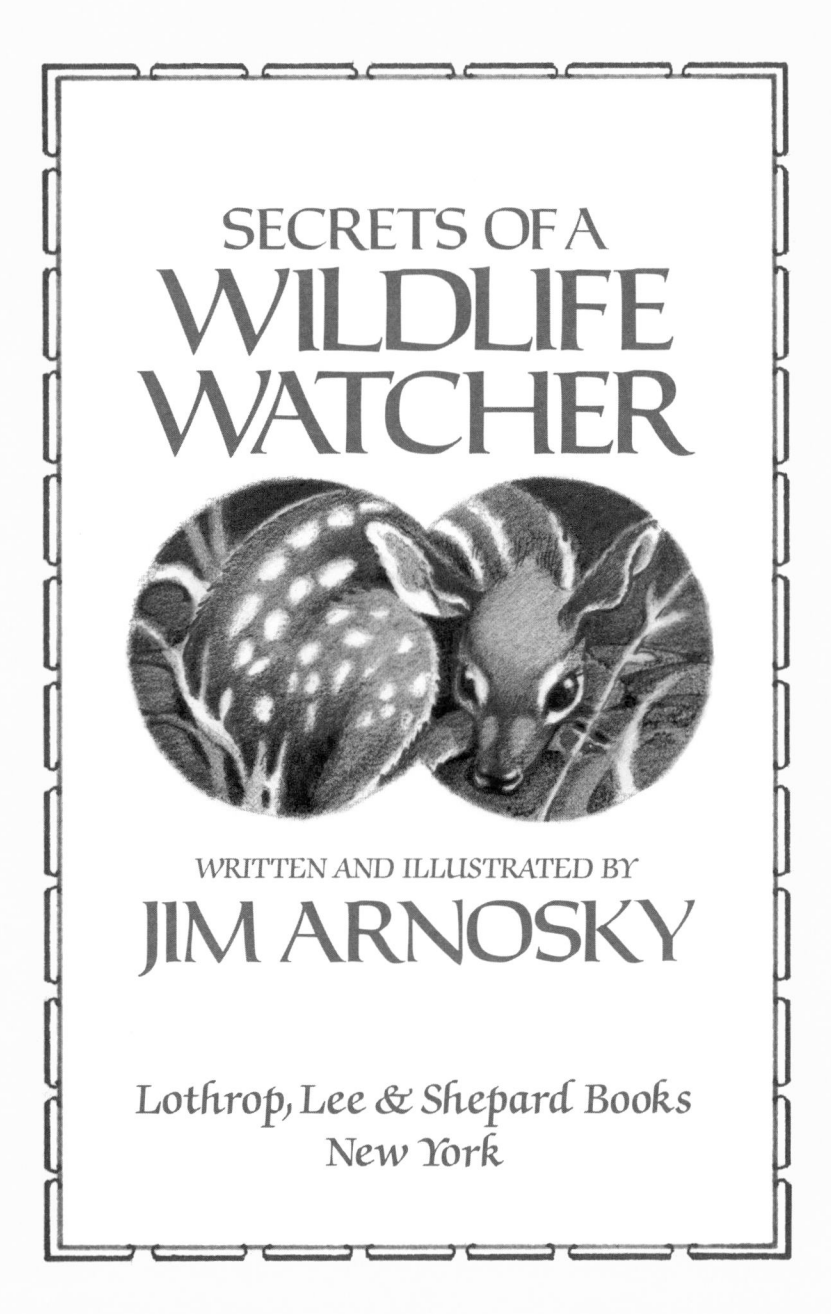

WRITTEN AND ILLUSTRATED BY

JIM ARNOSKY

Lothrop, Lee & Shepard Books
New York

Library of Congress Cataloging in Publication
Data. Arnosky, Jim. Secrets of a wildlife watcher.
Summary: Explains the techniques used in finding wild animals such as owls, turtles, squirrels,
foxes, beavers, and deer, and in getting close
enough to study their behavior. 1. Wildlife
watching—Juvenile literature. [1. Wildlife
watching. 2. Nature study. 3. Animals—Habits
and behavior] I. Title.
QL60.A76   1983   596'.00723   82-24920
ISBN 0-688-02079-8   ISBN 0-688-02081-X (lib. bdg.)

CONTENTS

Part I

FINDING

It was the first cold morning of winter. The ground was hard and coated with frost. I stepped briskly, following a deer path that skirted an open field. A deer had just been walking on the path. Its hoofprints were dark marks melted in the white frost. A sudden gust of bitterly cold wind whipped across the field, stinging my face. I pulled my coat collar up over my cheeks and nose. Just then I saw the deer! It was a doe standing about fifty feet ahead of me. She was pausing at a twiggy place along the path to nibble the slender branch tips. As she browsed, she turned and looked in my direction. I stopped completely still in my chilly tracks. The deer's thick coat was mostly winter gray. She had a white belly, a white patch under her chin, and a white circle around each eye. When she chewed, her breath condensed into tiny clouds in the freezing air. Another bitter gust blew over the field. I was shivering. The doe finished chewing her mouthful, then turned and continued on her way along the frosty path.

Whenever you see a wild animal, the chances are that you are in its home range. Animals are creatures of habit. They travel the same paths again and again. They know all the feeding areas, water sources, sleeping spots, and hiding places.

Many animals live out their entire lives in a very small area. A woodchuck rarely ventures more than two hundred feet from its burrow. A cottontail's whole world need be only a few acres. White-tailed deer are born, live, and die in an area of one square mile.

Different animals can have overlapping ranges. On one short hike in a wrinkle of a mountain, I found fresh tracks of fox, coyote, weasel, bobcat, and bear. All are predators. They are natural enemies, competing for available food. I'm sure they avoided meeting one another, but their tracks crossed, paralleled, and often followed the same trails.

TRACKS OF BLACK BEAR AND COYOTE I FOUND PRESSED SIDE BY SIDE IN THE MUD NEAR A MOUNTAIN SPRING

RED FOX ON
THE PROWL

A predator's home range is a hunting territory that it prowls over and over. A fox's hunting territory may cover one mile; a coyote's
two or three miles. A river otter's hunting territory can stretch to twenty miles around. It
takes the otter about twelve days to complete
the circuit. If you remember where you have
seen an animal once, you will eventually be
able to see it there again.

Last summer a trio of otters included the
pond behind my house in their hunting territory. Every two weeks I kept an eye on the
pond, expecting them to show up. They always did. From a hiding place on the bank I
watched them roll and twist acrobatically in
the water. When one would dive out of sight, I
would find it again by watching the line its
breath bubbles made on the surface. Often the
diver's wet head popped out of the water with
a gleaming trout clamped in its mouth. The otters always took trout in their front paws and
ate them like candy bars, head to tail, in big,
crunchy bites. Whenever they noticed me, all
three would duck under water and vamoose.

MARSH HAWK
AND SNAKE →

SPARROW HAWK
HOVERING
OVER PREY

Look for wildlife where water meets land, field meets wood, or lawn meets hedge. On these open "edges" sunlight stimulates a variety of plant growth that animals can eat while remaining near the safety of cover. This is why you often see animals along the roadside. They are attracted to the edges created by the road swath. The biggest white-tailed deer I've ever seen was standing on a roadside. It was a deep-bodied buck with eight long points on its antlers.

The wide ribbons of sunlit, brush-covered land on the sides of large highways are breeding grounds for small animals. Hawks take advantage of this and perch on trees, highway fencing, or road signs, and watch the ground for mice, squirrels, snakes, frogs, and songbirds. The next time you are riding in a car on a long trip, see how many hawks you can spot. Where prey animals are abundant, you may see a hawk perched along the highway every few miles or so. Learn to identify the various hawks you see.

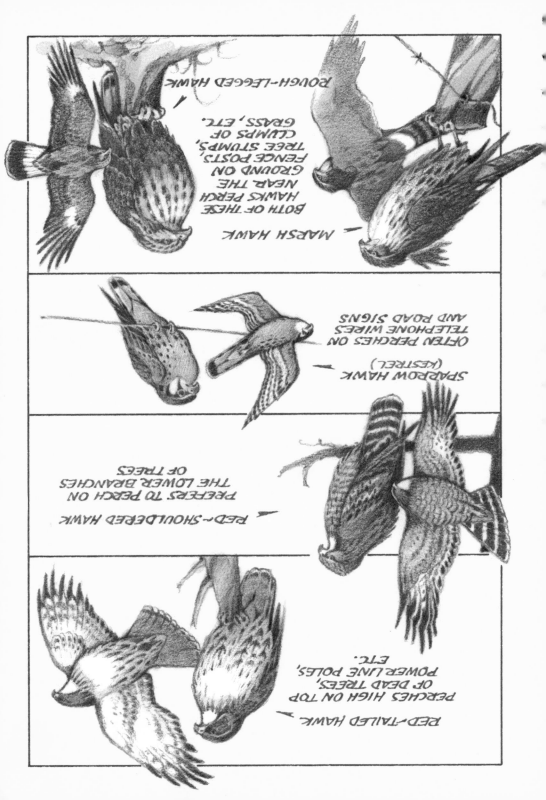

A hawk often shares its home range with an owl. The hawk hunts it during the day. The owl hunts at night. If you have a hawk living around you, you may also have a resident owl. One of the best ways to locate it in the daytime is to search the ground under evergreen trees for "owl pellets."

HERE ARE SOME SAMPLE PELLETS AND THE OWLS THAT PRODUCED THEM

GREAT HORNED OWL

LONG-EARED OWL

NOTE—HAWKS ALSO PRODUCE PELLETS. HAWK PELLETS ARE DIFFERENT FROM OWL PELLETS IN THAT, SINCE HAWKS CAN DIGEST BONES, THEIR PELLETS ARE NEARLY BONELESS

An owl often swallows its food whole. Undigestible bones and hair are eventually coughed up in the form of a pellet. This happens after the owl has roosted at the end of the night. When you find an owl's pellets, there is a good chance that the owl is sleeping in the tree above them. The size of the pellet is a clue to the size and type of owl you are looking for.

BARN OWL

SCREECH OWL

SAW-WHET OWL

ALL PELLETS ON THESE
PAGES ARE SHOWN
ACTUAL SIZE

RACCOON USING
A TRAIL

SQUIRREL
DIG

All wild animals leave telltale signs of their activities. Look for trails tramped along the ground. If you can bend over and walk along a trail without bumping into overhanging branches and twigs, you may be on a deer trail. If you must crawl to avoid being poked, the trail has been made by smaller animals, perhaps rabbits, foxes, raccoons, or skunks. Tiny inch-wide trails are pressed by the traveling feet of mice or voles.

Examine any digs, mounds, or scratches in the ground. A squirrel leaves a small dig where it has recovered a buried nut or seed. A skunk makes numerous little holes as it digs for grubs. A mole, tunneling close to the surface, creates a line of loosened earth and a small mound wherever it surfaces. Birds scratch ground debris away while searching for insects.

MOLE MOUND

STRIPPED
PINE CONE

Little piles of emptied nut shells or stripped pinecones are more squirrel signs. A scattering of disheveled feathers means a bird has been eaten there by a predator.

Slender branch tips and winter buds bitten off cleanly are the work of browsing deer or rabbits. Buds that have been eaten into but not bitten off the branch are chickadee peckings or the nibblings of climbing deer mice. Saplings whose bark has been gnawed are evidence of rabbits, mice, or porcupines.

A "girdle" of bare wood around the trunk of a large tree is a porcupine's doing. It has eaten all the bark from that spot. If a tree is chewed through and has fallen, you can be sure that you are in beaver territory. Beavers are the only wild animals that can fell trees.

RASPBERRY
BRANCH TIPS
BITTEN OFF

EVERGREEN
BUDS NIBBLED
INTO

A YELLOW BIRCH
GIRDLED BY
A PORCUPINE

ASPEN TREE
FELLED BY
A BEAVER

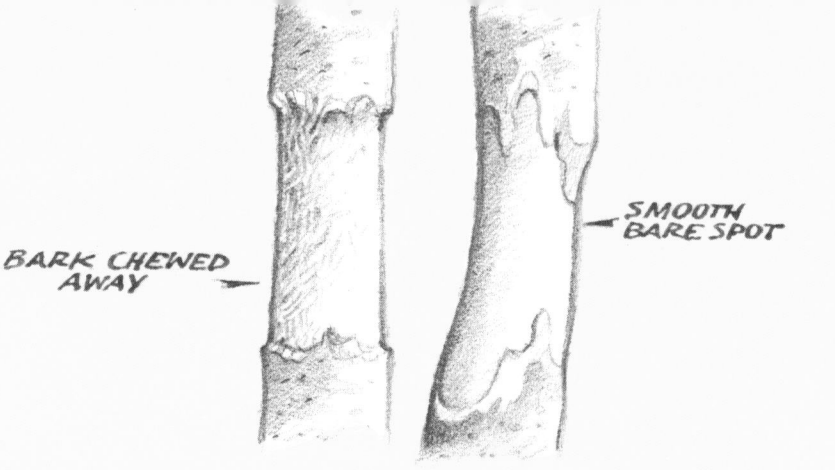

BARK CHEWED AWAY

SMOOTH BARE SPOT

A DOWNY WOODPECKER FEEDING ON ANTS UNDER LOOSE BARK

If tree bark has been stripped or rubbed off, you will find no chew marks in the smooth, bared wood. Smooth bare spots on trees may have been made by a deer peeling the bark to eat it or, during the autumn mating season, by a feisty buck's rubbing its antlers on the tree.

Woodpeckers peck into trees to find and eat wood-boring insects. As the birds hammer, they knock away chips of wood. Look for little pieces of wood scattered on the ground around a tree. Then look up for the holes the chips came from.

SAPSUCKERS DRILL SMALL HOLES IN HEALTHY TREES, THEN LATER RETURN TO EAT INSECTS ATTRACTED TO THE DRIPPING SAP

PILEATED WOODPECKERS MAKE RECTANGULAR HOLES DIGGING FOR WOOD BORING INSECT LARVAE

AN OPOSSUM
LIVING IN A
HOLLOW LOG
(LOOK FOR WHITE
OR SILVER HAIRS
ON LOG)

When you find a hole in a tree, never reach inside. It could be a den tree, and you may get bitten by an animal who lives there. Do, however, look closely around the hole entrance to see if any hairs are caught on the bark. They are proof that the hole is occupied.

The surest identifying signs that animals leave are their footprints. In winter I follow the activities of the birds, mice, rabbits, foxes, coyotes, dogs, and cats around our farm. Day after day they scribble their stories in the snow. Each new snowfall hides a chapter of their lives.

SQUIRRELS
WILL GNAW
AROUND THEIR
HOLE TO KEEP
IT FROM
GROWING
CLOSED

A TYPICAL
RACCOON
DEN TREE
(LOOK FOR BROWN
OR GRAY HAIRS
ON BARK)

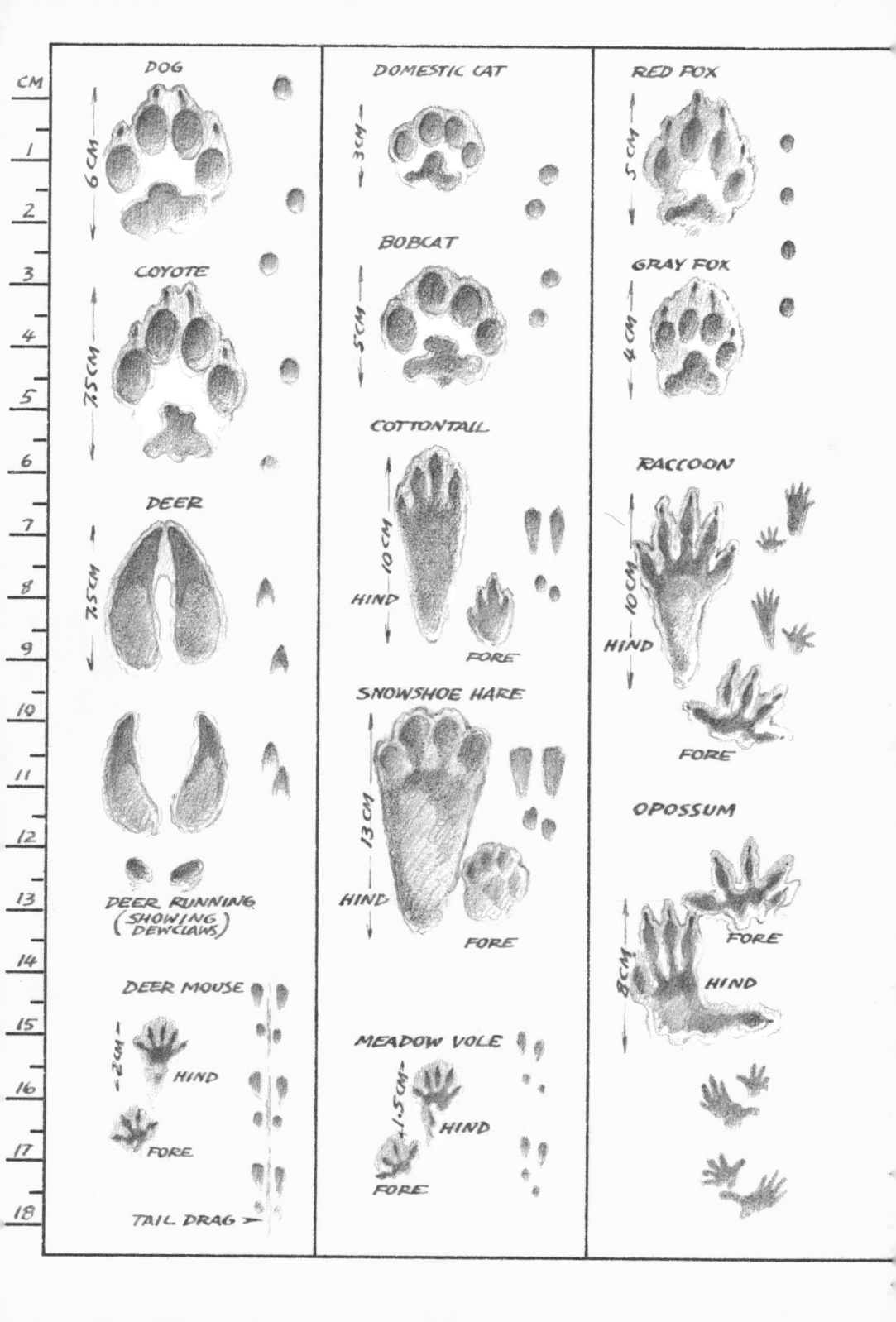

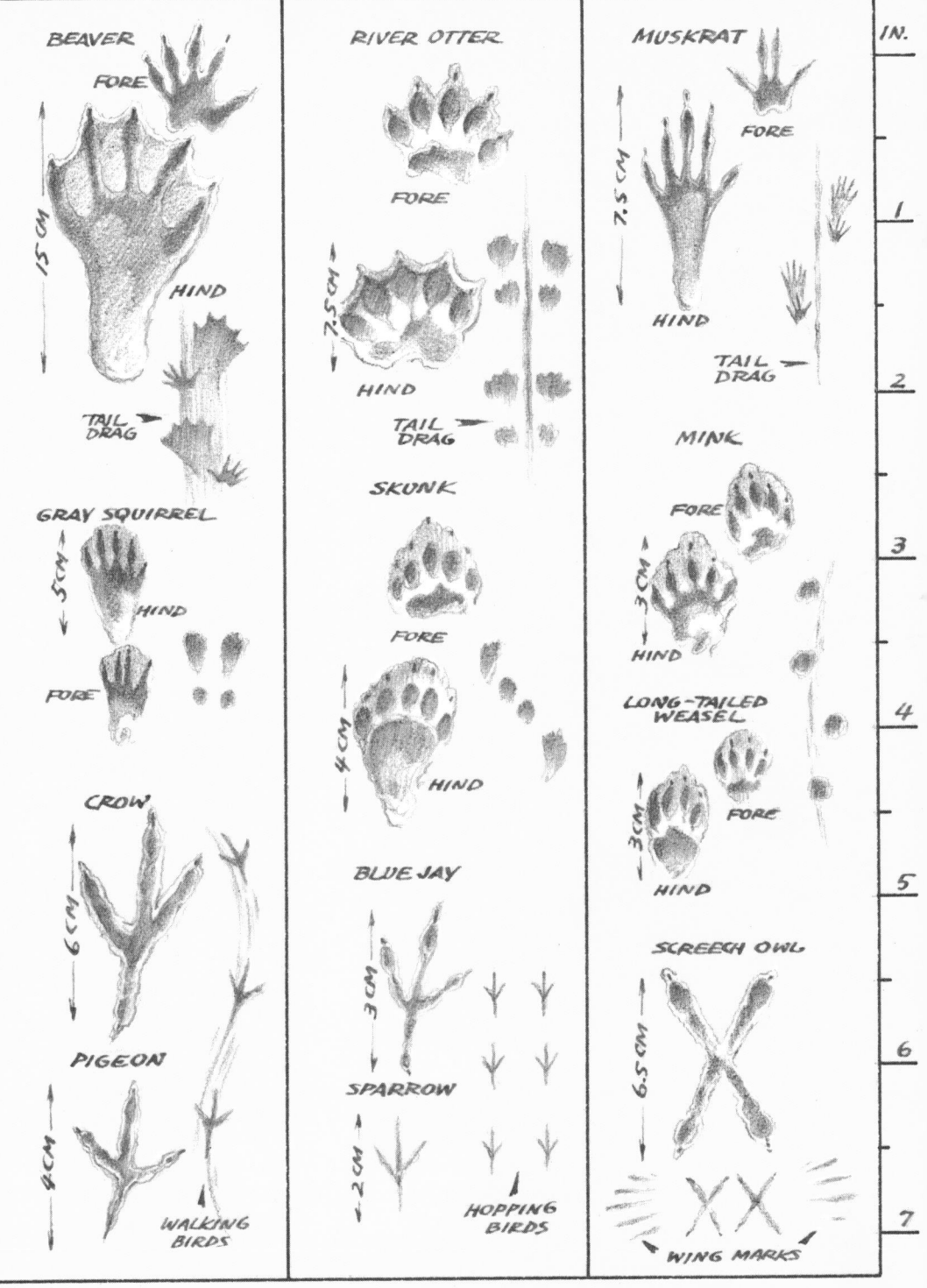

BEAVER
FORE
HIND
15 CM
TAIL DRAG

GRAY SQUIRREL
5 CM
HIND
FORE

CROW
6 CM

PIGEON
8 CM
WALKING BIRDS

RIVER OTTER
FORE
HIND
7.5 CM
TAIL DRAG

SKUNK
FORE
HIND
4 CM

BLUE JAY
3 CM

SPARROW
2 CM
HOPPING BIRDS

MUSKRAT
FORE
HIND
7.5 CM
TAIL DRAG

MINK
FORE
HIND
3 CM

LONG-TAILED WEASEL
FORE
HIND
3 CM

SCREECH OWL
6.5 CM
WING MARKS

IN.
1
2
3
4
5
6
7

NOTE: ALL TRACKS ARE SHOWN IN SNOW

An easy way to locate some of the nocturnal animals living in your area is to go outside after dark and listen for calls.

On clear winter nights coyotes howl from the chilly hilltops around our farm. Domestic dogs also do a lot of howling. Foxes make high-pitched yipping and yapping noises. Foxes also make a weird sound that resembles a cat crying.

Many people are familiar with the hoot of a great horned owl. What they may not realize is that the females have the deep, deep hoot. The males have a more highly pitched hoot.

Screech owls do not screech. They make a sound like a baby's cry. They also make a spooky, tremulous moan. If you hear a screech owl calling in the night woods, imitate the sound and call back. The little owl will answer and may even fly in closer to you.

OUR FARM "RAMTAILS" IN WINTER

Animals come out of hiding to eat. The more you learn about their feeding habits, the easier it will be to predict when they will be afoot. For a wild animal, staying alive depends on how alert its senses are to the approach of danger. When an animal is feeding it is vulnerable to danger. Its eyes are busy looking at what it is eating. The smell of food fills its nostrils, and its own chewing noises drown out all other sounds. This is why wild animals are so high strung while they are eating. All their muscles are tense and ready to react to any surprise.

For the sake of safety, prey animals visit feeding spots for short periods at a time. Birds and squirrels snatch seeds and run to safety to eat them. A deer limits its time at feeding areas by quickly chewing and swallowing as much food as it can fit in its "paunch"—the first compartment of a deer's four-compartment stomach. Then it moves to cover and brings the food up in a wad to chew again, this time more thoroughly. Whenever you see a deer "chewing its cud," you know it feels safe and secure. By the time food has passed through all four compartments of a deer's stomach, every ounce of nutrition has been squeezed from it. This reduces the amount of feeding a deer has to do.

A WHITE-TAILED DEER
CHEWING HER CUD

LARGE, OPEN
FEEDERS
WORK BEST

WILD ANIMALS
LIKE LOTS OF
"ELBOW ROOM"

WIRE
HOOK

ONION BAG
FILLED WITH
SOUP BONES
OR SUET

Rabbits get the utmost from the food they eat. When a rabbit visits a feeding spot, it grazes fast, eating as much food as possible. Later, in the safety of cover, the rabbit's body begins producing special droppings formed from the recently grazed food. These first droppings are re-eaten for remaining nutrients. This stretches one meal into two, and limits dangerous trips to grazing areas.

When you see an animal gathering food, you have discovered one of its regular feeding spots. If the area has plenty of food available, you can be sure the animal will return again and again, at approximately the same time each day. Once you learn an animal's feeding routine, you can show up a little ahead of it and watch from a distance.

Setting up a winter bird feeder is a good way to invite wildlife out in the open to be watched. Animals are opportunists. They can't pass up an easy meal. A well-stocked feeder will attract squirrels, chipmunks, and mice, as well as birds. Predators also visit feeders to nab unsuspecting seed eaters.

COAT HANGER AND
SUET LOG FEEDER

NOTE: LOCATE YOUR
FEEDER NEAR SOME
TREES OR BRUSH SO
BIRDS CAN FLY TO
SAFETY

DRILLED HOLES
FILLED WITH SUET

A CAT CACHE

A CAT BURIES ITS CACHES
USING ITS FRONT PAWS ~
LOOK FOR RAKE MARKS
FROM CAT CLAWS

(CATS ALSO BURY THEIR DROPPINGS)

Most predators begin hunting at dusk and prowl until dawn. When prey is plentiful, foxes, coyotes, bobcats, and bears may eat only a small portion of each animal they kill. They hide the rest and go hunting for more. Food hidden this way is called a "cache" (pronounced *cash*). A predator's territory can have many such caches. They are the hunter's buried treasures. Caches are quite important to wildlife watchers because the animals who make them return from time to time to check up on them.

I once watched a red fox hunting in a field of fresh-mown hay. The cutting must have disrupted the entire meadow's mouse population, and the fox was making the most of their confusion. It pranced down the raked rows, pouncing on any movement or sound made in the drying hay. Each time it killed a mouse, the fox cached it and romped away to find another.

A FOX CACHE

A CANINE BURIES ITS
CACHES USING ITS NOSE
TO PUSH DIRT, DEBRIS,
OR SNOW OVER THE
FOOD IT IS HIDING

TRACKS AROUND A CACHE ARE CLUES
TO ITS MAKER

Foxes have another interesting habit that is important for a wildlife watcher to know. They like to sleep in an open area on an elevated spot where they can see, hear, and smell everything around them. In winter you can spot a fox sleeping in a field when its red fur stands out against snow-covered ground. At all other times of the year a fox's color is camouflaged against earthen browns.

Wild animals blend into their surroundings so well that often we notice them only when they are moving. Scanning a view for any slight movement is one way to pick out camouflaged animals. Look for the stomping leg or swiveling ear of an anxious deer. Search for the twitching nose of a nervous rabbit. Squirrels often flick their tails. Small birds can't stay still very long. Watch for them flitting from branch to branch.

USING YOUR HANDS
TO NARROW YOUR
FIELD OF VIEW

Sometimes it helps to scan an area with your hands held around your eyes like binoculars. This narrows your concentration to a limited area and even magnifies the area slightly. I never use real binoculars for finding wildlife. I believe they are too limiting. I always locate wildlife with my naked eyes. Then, if I have binoculars, I use them to "zoom in" for a closer look.

If you are watching a moving animal and it suddenly seems to disappear before your eyes . . . it may simply have stopped and blended into the scene. Look over the spot where you last saw the animal. Often you will find it again, standing still and watching you!

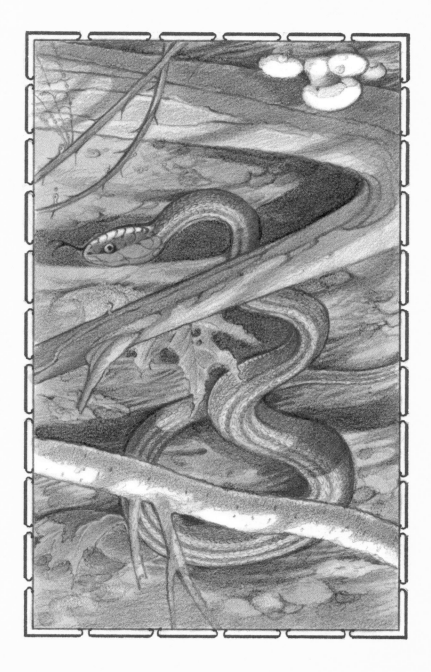

Part II
STALKING

The woods were rain-soaked. Soil gurgled under the press of my footsteps. I walked a familiar trail, wide-eyed for a glimpse of wildlife. Ahead, something moved on the soggy leaves. It was a little snake! I tried to get a closer look, but it scooted behind a fallen tree branch. I approached again, very slowly, and knelt a few feet from the broken branch. The snake didn't move. It was an olive-colored garter snake with bright yellow stripes down its back. Each of its scales was "keeled" in the center by a raised line. The snake's eyes looked like polished stones. They made me wonder what they were seeing. Its delicate head was jade green and its mouth was white. A tiny forked tongue flicked out. It was wine red.

The little snake had sensed my approach and was seeking cover when I spotted it. Once behind the branch it felt hidden, so it stayed, even when I came near. One secret to getting close to small, shy animals is to let them find cover before trying to approach them.

Wild animals are sensitive to everything around them. Stalking them takes practice and patience. In reptiles, fish, and mammals, the sense of smell is acute. A snake depends on its sense of smell to locate food and detect danger. A salmon can smell a bear in the water a mile upstream. A fox can sniff a rabbit's scent in tracks that are days old.

Wherever you go you leave some of your scent in microscopic molecules that are re-

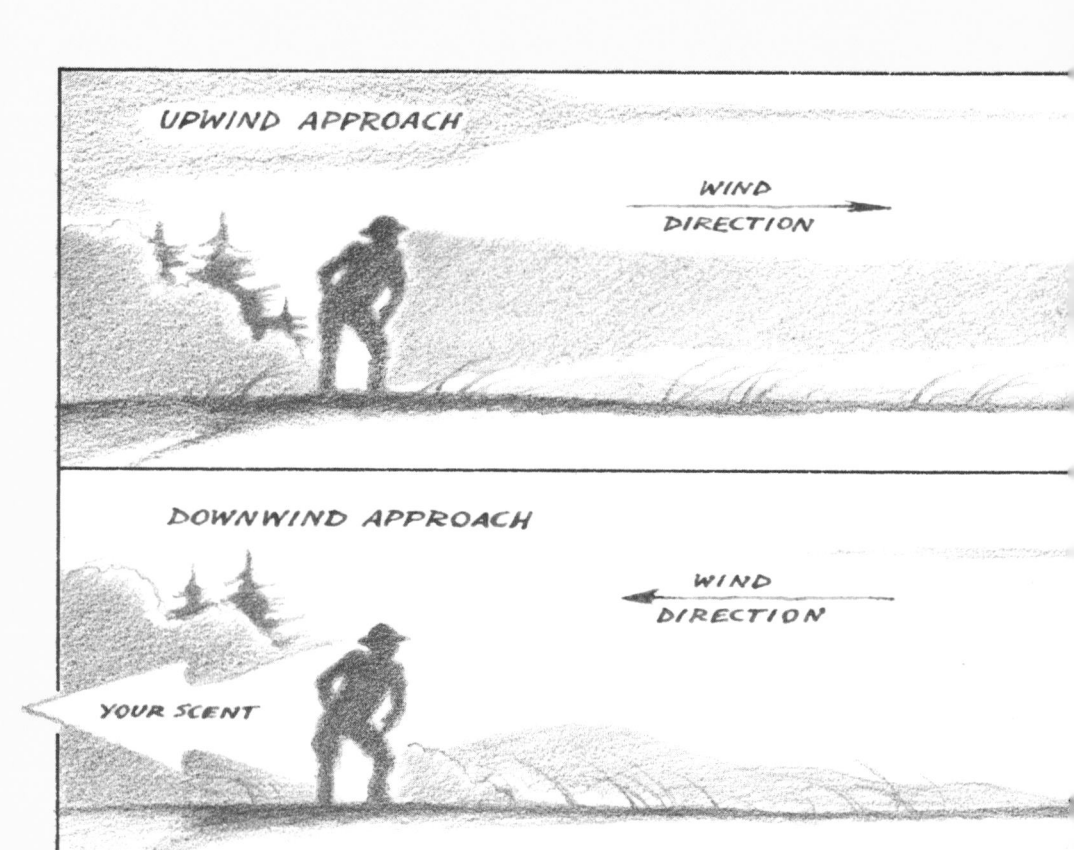

leased from your body and clothing. These molecules fall to the ground as you move. They cling to vegetation. They float in the air and drift to surrounding areas. Often your scent reaches an animal long before you do, which scares it away. When you see a wild animal, stay downwind. This will keep your scent in back of you and away from the animal you are watching.

YOUR SCENT

MANY ANIMALS, LIKE
THIS RABBIT, CAN SWIVEL
THEIR EARS TO PICK UP
SOUNDS FROM VARIOUS
DIRECTIONS

EARS FORWARD   EARS BACKWARD

Most animals can hear as well as they can smell. Even snakes, fish, and others deaf to airborne sounds can feel noises vibrating through the ground. When stalking wildlife, be as quiet as possible. Step softly. Try not to scrape against trees or brush. If you must make a sound, do so when the animal you are watching is busy chewing food, shifting position, or moving to a new spot. It will be making noises of its own and may not notice yours. If you are heard and the animal becomes alert—freeze in your tracks!

A SNAKE
FEELS SOUND
VIBRATIONS
WITH THE PART
OF ITS BODY
THAT TOUCHES
GROUND

Keep still and most animals will not see you, even if you are out in the open. In general, animals look out for movements. Many animals, including most mammals, see only in shades of gray. A motionless figure is difficult for them to single out of a scene. Sometimes the shape of a standing human, still or moving, will frighten them. You can disguise your human shape simply by crouching down.

SOUNDS VIBRATE THROUGH
A FISH'S SKULL TO AN
INTERNAL EAR INSIDE
THE FISH'S HEAD

THE LATERAL ORGAN ALONG A
FISH'S SIDES SENSES SLOW
(SOUNDLESS) MOVEMENTS
IN THE WATER

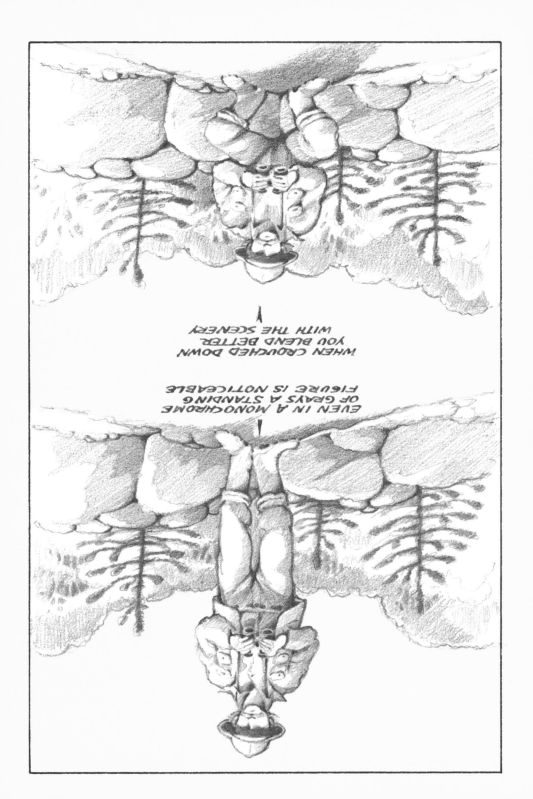

EVEN IN A MONOCHROME OF GRAYS A STANDING FIGURE IS NOTICEABLE

WHEN CROUCHED DOWN YOU BLEND BETTER WITH THE SCENERY

ANIMALS WITH POOR
VISION – LIKE BEAVERS,
MUSKRATS, AND SKUNKS –
WILL NOT SEE YOU
UNLESS YOU MOVE

A BEAVER ON ALERT

I was once crouched downwind from a beaver who was working away on its dam. At times the busy engineer was less than ten feet from me. It rolled some heavy stones to the dam site and shoved them into place with the side of its strong body. I could hear the stones squish into the mud on the dam. In my motionless crouch, I was invisible. After a while, though, my legs became stiff and I had to stand and stretch them. Instantly, the beaver saw me and disappeared under water with a loud splash of its flat tail.

Birds do see in color and rely mainly on eyesight for survival. They can see both near and far objects much better than other animals can.

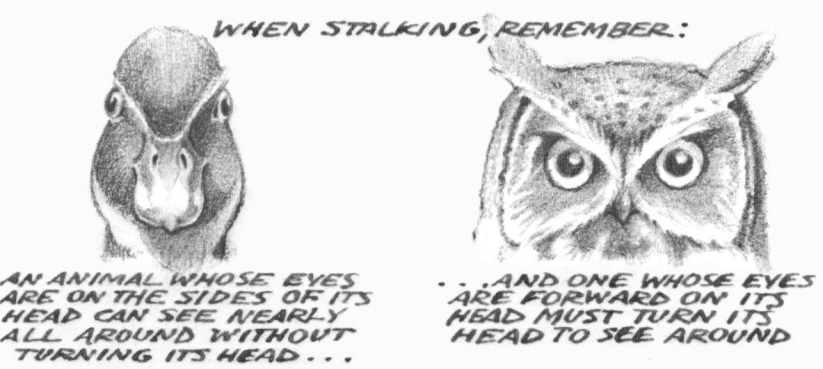

WHEN STALKING, REMEMBER:

AN ANIMAL WHOSE EYES
ARE ON THE SIDES OF ITS
HEAD CAN SEE NEARLY
ALL AROUND WITHOUT
TURNING ITS HEAD . . .

. . .AND ONE WHOSE EYES
ARE FORWARD ON ITS
HEAD MUST TURN ITS
HEAD TO SEE AROUND

MOST BIRDS CAN WATCH
ABOVE FOR DANGER...

...WHILE SEARCHING
BELOW FOR FOOD

A sparrow's eyes can be focused on a seed right near its beak one instant, then focused on a distant cat the next. The images birds see are clearly defined. Soaring birds see things up to eight times more sharply than humans do. This is why a hawk high in the sky can spot a mouse running on the ground.

Because birds have such exquisite eyesight, they are difficult to approach. Bird watchers use binoculars to study birds. One way to watch them up close without using binoculars is to go to a place they frequent, sit still, keep quiet, and wait until they arrive. Soon they will be going about their bird business all around you.

THE SIGHT OF STARING EYES
CAN STARTLE ANIMALS—
ESPECIALLY BIRDS

A BRIMMED HAT
WILL SHADE AND
HIDE YOUR EYES

THE JOY OF STALKING IS GETTING UP CLOSE ENOUGH TO WATCH ANIMALS ACTING NATURALLY

IF YOU GET TOO CLOSE ANIMALS WILL ACT TENSE AND UNNATURAL

It is possible to get too close to the animals you are watching. Always keep at a distance that is comfortable for them and for you. Do not disturb nesting birds. And *never* approach an animal that is with its young. Wild animal parents can be ferociously protective. If you come upon a baby animal that looks orphaned, let it be. Mother may be watching you from a hiding place nearby. Do not touch or corner a wild animal, and never follow an animal into unfamiliar places. There is no such thing as a tame wild animal. Be wary of any that seem fearless of you. They could be sick and dangerous.

During mating season male members of the deer tribe become irritable and unpredictable. They do not tolerate anything that gets in their way as they seek out a mate. Last October I saw a bull moose crossing a farm meadow. It appeared calm and unhurried. But when the farmer's cows approached to get a closer look at their ungainly visitor, the moose lowered its antlers and charged them. It happened very quickly. The cows scattered and the moose continued on its way, in search of a mate. All deer mate in autumn. Remember to avoid male deer during this time.

VERY YOUNG FAWNS ARE ODORLESS. THIS PROTECTS THEM FROM PREDATORS. MOTHER DEER STAY AWAY (EXCEPT WHEN NURSING) SO THEIR OWN SCENT WILL NOT MARK THEIR FAWNS' HIDING PLACES

The safest way to get a close look at animals you would rather not go near is to use binoculars. Through my binoculars I've watched moose, wild ponies, poisonous snakes, alligators, skunks, and porcupines.

Carrying a pair of binoculars can add an intimacy to all your wildlife watching. Through these lenses the delicate details of animal anatomy are magnified. With a turn of a dial individual scales, feathers, hairs, and whiskers come into focus.

ALWAYS FIND WILDLIFE WITH YOUR NAKED EYES

Any pair of binoculars can be "set" to your own eyesight. First, look through them at some object and turn the center focus dial until the object looks as clear as possible. Then close your right eye. Look at the object with only your left eye and turn the left eyepiece to sharpen the focus. Next close your left eye. Look at the object with only your right eye and focus the right eyepiece. You'll have to do this only once. From then on all you'll have to adjust is the center focus dial.

THEN USE BINOCULARS TO GET A CLOSER LOOK

CENTER FOCUS DIAL

LEFT EYEPIECE   RIGHT EYEPIECE

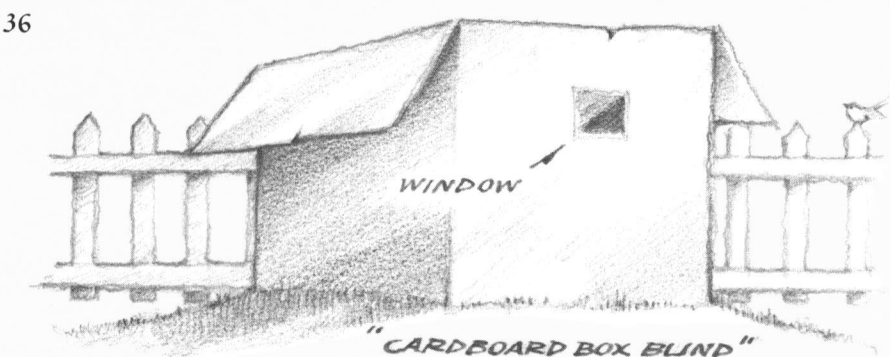

"CARDBOARD BOX BLIND"

Another way to get close to wild animals is to set up a "blind" in their midst. A blind is something you can hide inside and see out of. It can be as plain as a cardboard box with peepholes or as fancy as a nylon tent with zippered windows. To get close to their shy subjects, some wildlife photographers construct elaborate blinds that resemble natural objects. Photography blinds have been made to imitate brushpiles, cattail islands, and muskrat lodges. I use a simple portable blind made of green burlap.

"POP-UP TENT BLIND"
WITH
ZIPPERED WINDOWS

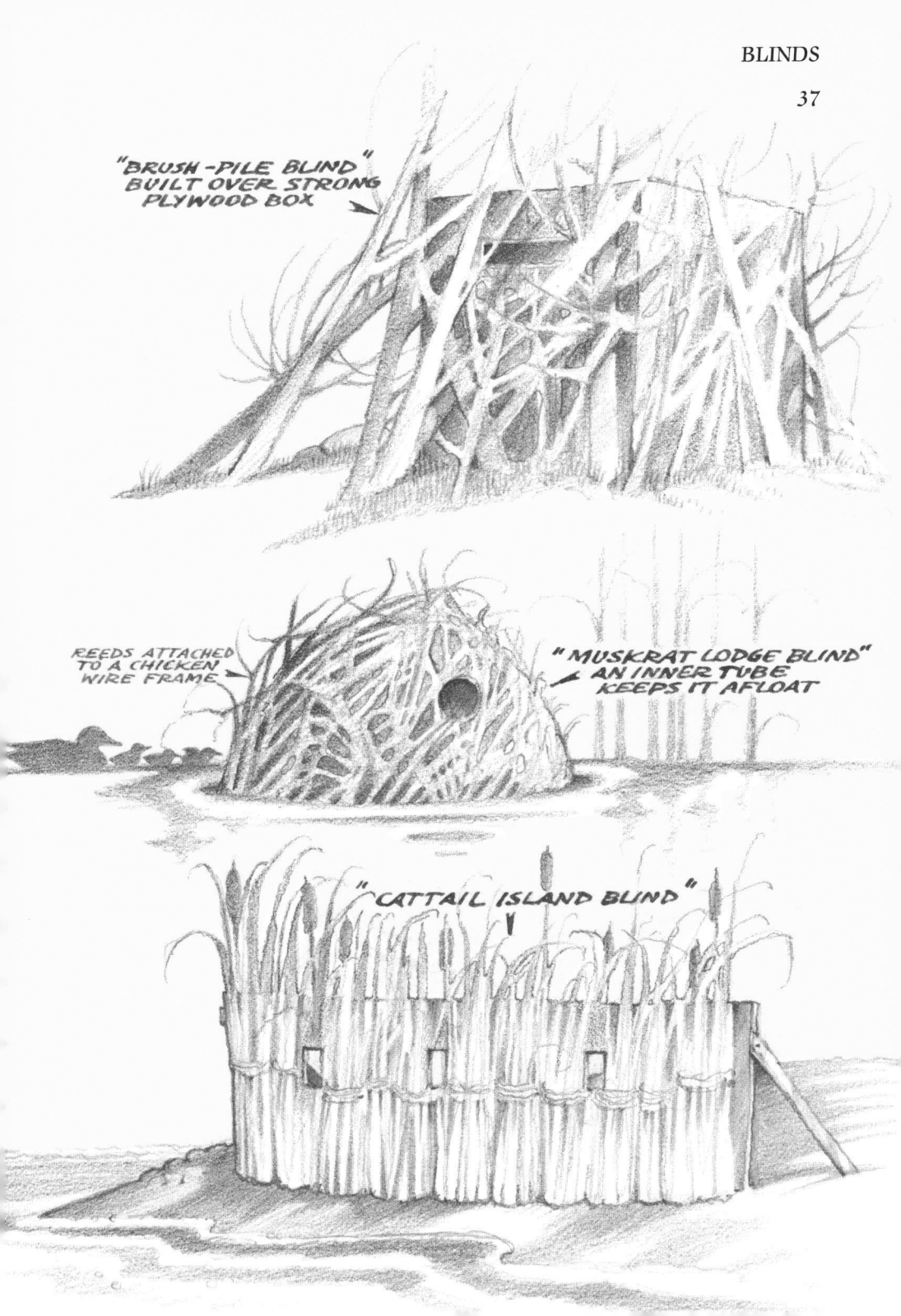

"BRUSH-PILE BLIND"
BUILT OVER STRONG
PLYWOOD BOX

REEDS ATTACHED
TO A CHICKEN
WIRE FRAME

"MUSKRAT LODGE BLIND"
AN INNER TUBE
KEEPS IT AFLOAT

"CATTAIL ISLAND BLIND"

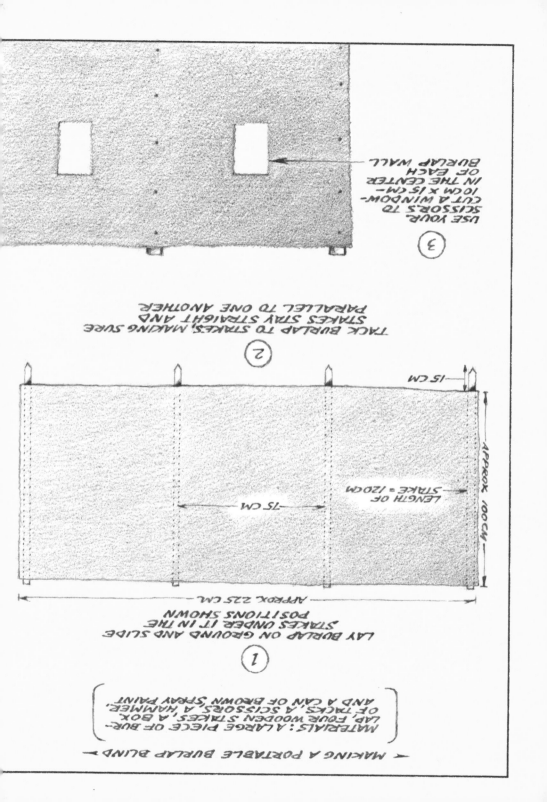

◄ MAKING A PORTABLE BURLAP BLIND ►

MATERIALS: A LARGE PIECE OF BUR-
LAP, FOUR WOODEN STAKES, A BOX
OF TACKS, A SCISSORS, A HAMMER,
AND A CAN OF BROWN SPRAY PAINT.

1. LAY BURLAP ON GROUND AND SLIDE
STAKES UNDER IT IN THE
POSITIONS SHOWN

APPROX 225 CM.

APPROX 100 CM

LENGTH OF STAKE = 120CM

75 CM

15 CM

2. TACK BURLAP TO STAKES, MAKING SURE
STAKES STAY STRAIGHT AND
PARALLEL TO ONE ANOTHER

3. USE YOUR
SCISSORS TO
CUT A WINDOW-
10CM X 15 CM-
IN THE CENTER
OF EACH
BURLAP WALL.

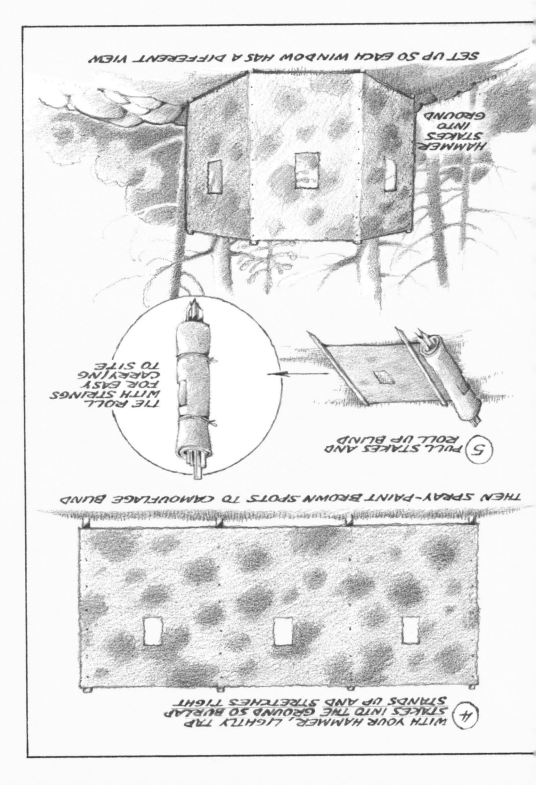

SET UP SO EACH WINDOW HAS A DIFFERENT VIEW

HAMMER STAKES INTO GROUND

TIE ROLL WITH STRINGS FOR EASY CARRYING TO SITE

5) PULL STAKES AND ROLL UP BLIND

THEN SPRAY-PAINT BROWN SPOTS TO CAMOUFLAGE BLIND

4) WITH YOUR HAMMER, LIGHTLY TAP STAKES INTO THE GROUND SO BURLAP STANDS UP AND STRETCHES TIGHT

WHEN POSSIBLE, SET UP
YOUR BLIND NEAR WATER.
EVEN THE SLIGHTEST
TRICKLE OF WATER
ATTRACTS WILDLIFE.

Wherever you set up your blind, the animals in the area will need time to get used to it. Leave it alone for a day or two. The wildlife will inspect the blind and eventually accept it as part of the scenery.

Be sneaky while walking to your blind. While you are in it, be quiet. Always try to enter and leave when wildlife activity is slow. Remember to carry something to snack on and a book to read while waiting for animals to come by. Bring your binoculars. If you are an artist or writer, pack a notebook and pencils. Take along a camera and keep it handy.

BARK BEETLE

YOUR BLIND ITSELF
WILL ATTRACT SMALL
ANIMALS. LOOK FOR
THEM. LEARN WHICH
KINDS THEY ARE.

WOOLLY BEAR
CATERPILLAR

AMERICAN
TOAD

RED-BACKED
SALAMANDER

LEAST SHREW

One crisp autumn day I was sitting in my blind while a doe and her two grown summer fawns were grazing in the field in front of me. I pushed my camera lens through the blind's little window to take their picture. Slowly I cocked the shutter. The camera's sound alerted the doe. She stared at my blind and began walking toward it. I held my camera ready. The doe kept coming closer. She was curious. Her big eyes were glued to the shiny lens of my camera. I was beginning to think she was going to walk right up to my blind and hop inside with me when she stopped abruptly about eight feet away. My finger was trembling on the shutter button. I turned the focus dial with my other hand to sharpen the deer's image, pressed the shutter—*click*—and got her picture!

Part III
WATCHING

The snapping turtle clambered over the stubs of last year's corn, passing row after row before finding a spot that suited her. Then, turning and facing her own trail from the pond, she began making a nest hole in the soft spring soil. When she had dug as deep as her hind legs could reach, she began to lay her eggs. Each egg was pure white and as round as a Ping-Pong ball. They appeared one at a time, like doves from a magician's coat. Each was guided carefully into the sandy hole by the turtle's hind feet. After the last egg rolled gently into the nest, she buried the batch by pushing dirt over them with her body. She smoothed the spot with her bottom shell, then followed her tracks back to the water.

I stared at the spot of freshly worked earth and thought of the baby turtles that would develop and hatch there in sun-warmed ground. I looked to the pond and wondered if the snapping turtle had already forgotten her hidden eggs in the cornfield, because, if she had, the secret was all mine.

MAYFLY NYMPH
SWIMMING TO
THE SURFACE

When you witness an intimate tidbit of a wild animal's private life, glean all you can from the experience. Pay attention to the details, and wonder about what you see. Exercise your eyesight. Don't just look. Observe. Note an animal's size and color. Watch how it moves. Learn exactly what it is doing.

WINGED FLY
BREAKING
OUT OF ITS
NYMPHAL
SKIN

You can always be sharpening your powers of observation. For example, while casting for bass in a nearby pond, I noticed the sudden emergence of hundreds of very large green mayflies from the water. Some were in their nymphal stage, swimming from the pond's bottom up to the surface. Some had broken through their nymphal skins, and their new, winged bodies were shimmying and squirming out. Others had completely shucked their old skins and were floating on the pond's surface waiting for their wings to

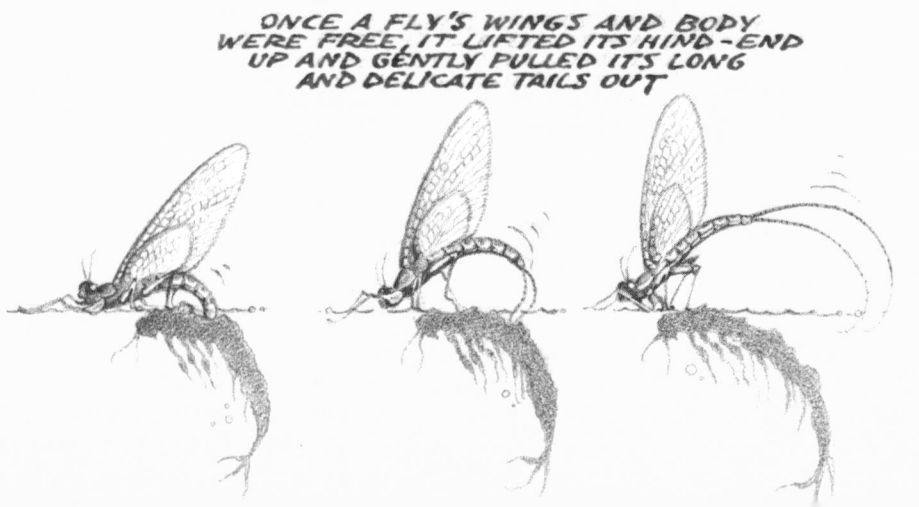

ONCE A FLY'S WINGS AND BODY
WERE FREE, IT LIFTED ITS HIND-END
UP AND GENTLY PULLED ITS LONG
AND DELICATE TAILS OUT

dry. As soon as they could, they flew off the water away from the jaws of feeding fish. The bass in the pond were splashing loudly, snatching every swimming nymph and floating fly they saw. One bass took my own imitation fly and ended up in my net. I was unhooking the fish when I discovered that its throat was jammed full of mayflies. There were even some hanging out of the sides of its mouth.

The surface activity continued. I began to challenge my eyes to see if I could freeze in my mind the sight of a feeding fish the moment it jumped after a mayfly. One large bass poked its head out of the water right near a floating fly. For an instant the green-backed fish paused, like a sea serpent terrorizing a sailing vessel. Then it lunged forward and gulped the mayfly down.

ADULT
GREAT HORNED
OWLS

APPROX. 61 CM

♀

APPROX. 51 CM

♂

Many male birds are easily recognized by their brilliant colors and well-defined markings, while the females are camouflaged with a mottling of earth hues. Even in bird species where the two sexes look similar, the females are plainer looking than the males. There are a few exceptions. Male and female owls and hawks are identical in color and markings. However, the females are noticeably bigger than their male counterparts. In the case of kingfishers, females are actually more colorful than the males! The female kingfisher has a festive-looking red breastband, which the male lacks.

All baby birds have large, brightly-colored mouths. When opened wide they form targets for busy parents, who must work nonstop to keep the babies fed. Young birds can be recognized by their large mouths for some time, even after they have left the nest.

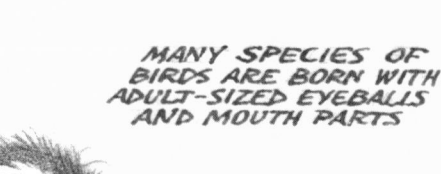

MANY SPECIES OF BIRDS ARE BORN WITH ADULT-SIZED EYEBALLS AND MOUTH PARTS

← BABY ROBINS

♂ IS THE SYMBOL FOR MALE   ♀ IS THE SYMBOL FOR FEMALE

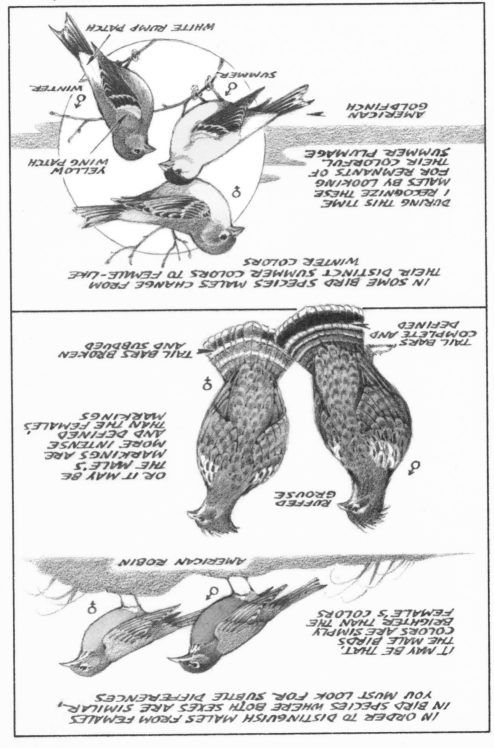

A FEMALE TOAD
CARRYING
TWO MALES

EARDRUM

♂

BULLFROGS

♀

Female frogs and toads are larger than males. Toad females are so much bigger than males that they look comical together. In a springtime breeding area it is common to see a huge toad carrying one or two smaller toads "piggyback." The huge toad is a female, and her dwarfish riders are males trying to mate with her.

The size difference between males and females is less obvious in frogs. But in the case of the bullfrog and green frog, males can be recognized at a glance. Their eardrums are larger than their eyes.

During breeding season, male frogs and toads sing. When singing they inflate a vocal

THE SOUND OF A MALE'S SONG WILL ATTRACT A FEMALE TO HIS AREA. ONCE SHE IS NEARBY, THE SIGHT OF HIS "THROAT BALLOON" ALSO HELPS GUIDE HER TO HIM.

A MALE TOAD SINGING IN MOONLIGHT

A WAD OF FROG EGGS
(ACTUAL SIZE)

STRINGS OF TOAD EGGS
(ACTUAL SIZE)

sac that resonates the sound. In many species of frogs and toads the vocal sac, when inflated, forms a balloon under the singer's chin. Look for these "throat balloons" along the water's edge when you hear frogs or toads singing.

The eggs of most frogs and toads are deposited in water. Frog eggs are usually all stuck together in a wad or flat mass. Toad eggs are in long gelatinous strings. Both frogs and toads hatch as legless, tailed tadpoles. Tadpoles have fishlike mouths and gills. Toad tadpoles are tiny and black. They develop into tiny toadlets. Most frog tadpoles are greenish and, in many species, grow to be as large as their parents before transforming into frogs. When you see a large frog tadpole, look for other signs of metamorphosis such as developing legs, bulging eyes, and a widening mouth.

TOAD TADPOLE

TOADLET

BULLFROG TADPOLES

DEVELOPING LEGS

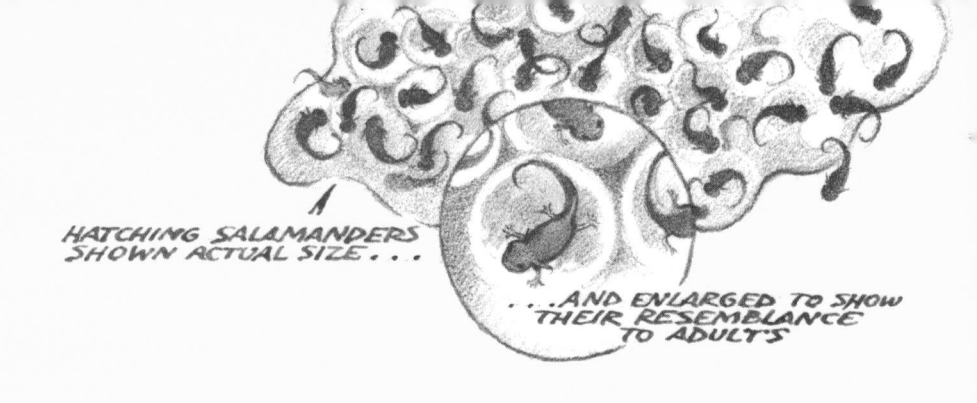

HATCHING SALAMANDERS
SHOWN ACTUAL SIZE . . .

. . . AND ENLARGED TO SHOW
THEIR RESEMBLANCE
TO ADULTS

While hunting for tadpoles in a woodland pool, I once came across a wriggling mass of hatching salamanders. I got down on my knees and looked as closely as I could without touching them with my nose. From a distance hatched salamanders look like tadpoles. They are actually tiny, gill-breathing versions of their parents.

Most salamanders are secretive, solitary, and rarely seen unless accidentally discovered. My favorite salamander, the red-spotted newt, lives the first few years of its life as a shy orange woods-dwelling salamander called an eft. But once it reaches breeding age it migrates to water and lives the rest of its life as a green aquatic salamander called a newt. Newts are not shy or secretive. They live in the open, sunny shallows of ponds and lakes. They are easy to see and great fun to watch.

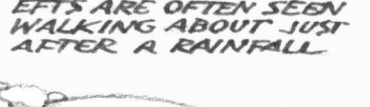

EFTS ARE OFTEN SEEN
WALKING ABOUT JUST
AFTER A RAINFALL

HEAVY WITH
EGGS

♂

♀

CLASPING
PADS

HIND LEGS ARE
SMALLER THAN MALE'S

During springtime I recognize male newts by their "clasping pads." Sand-textured clasping pads on the legs and feet are common on the breeding males of many amphibians. These pads, along with strong grasping limbs, help the males hold on to the slippery females.

Male turtles have concave bottom shells. This helps keep mating males from sliding off the females' top shells. But you can tell a box turtle's gender without turning it over to look at its bottom shell. Male box turtles have bright red eyes. Females have brown.

Young turtles have rounder, more domed shells than their parents. They also are more vivid in color. The older a turtle gets, the duller its colors become. Its markings grow less defined.

♀

FLAT OR
CONVEX

♂

CONCAVE

BABY
BOX TURTLE

IF YOU FIND A BABY BOX TURTLE YOU WILL BE IN VERY SPECIAL COMPANY. THE FAMED WILDLIFE WATCHER, LEONARD LEE RUE III TOLD ME THAT EVEN THOUGH ADULT BOX TURTLES ARE THE MOST COMMONLY SEEN TURTLES — BABY BOX TURTLES ARE RARELY SEEN. IN MR. RUE'S WHOLE LIFE HE HAS ONLY SEEN FIVE BABY BOX TURTLES!

Only male deer, elk, and moose have antlers. They grow new ones each year. Each stage of antler development is a visible identifying mark on a male's head. In spring, look for small bumps where antlers are beginning to grow. They are nourished all summer by a covering of velvety tissue. During this time they look fat and nubby. By summer's end the "velvet" dries up and peels. I've seen it hanging in shreds from a deer's antlers. Male deer practice for autumn mating fights by sparring with small trees. This rubbing scrapes off the remaining velvet and sharpens antler points. At first the bare antlers look red and bloody,

THIS CHART SHOWS AN EXAMPLE OF ONE MALE WHITE-TAILED DEER'S ANTLER DEVELOPMENT DURING ONE YEAR.

SPRING
NEW ANTLERS BEGIN

SUMMER
ANTLERS GROW INSIDE "VELVET" COVERING

NOTE: SIZE OF ANTLERS AND NUMBER OF POINTS DEPEND ON

but eventually the deer's rubbing polishes them white. Finally, in winter, antlers drop off, leaving visible, light-colored bare spots on the deer's head. Here spring's new antlers will begin.

Deer are the only mammals whose males and females can be identified easily on sight. You can only make an educated guess at the gender of other mammals. Just remember that mammal males are *generally* bigger and brawnier than mammal females. Males are often loners. Also, if you see a mammal with young, the parent is a female.

VELVET REMNANT

BARE PEDICELS

AUTUMN
ANTLERS RUBBED CLEAN

WINTER
ANTLERS DROPPED

A DEER'S HEREDITY, AGE, NOURISHMENT, AND STATE OF HEALTH

MALLARD DUCKLINGS

Mammals are naturally curious. From birth they embark on an adventure of discovery. When you are watching an animal with its young, take special note of the enthusiasm with which the youngsters approach each new object and situation.

Mammals retain their curiosity all their lives. I once watched as an adult raccoon investigated my drawing case and its contents. The raccoon's nimble fingers removed and examined every pencil and pen. Each eraser was felt, sniffed, and tasted. I later lost that same drawing case while sketching at the zoo. My subject, a curious elephant, reached out with its trunk and probed the case while I drew. Before I knew it, the case had disappeared into the elephant's mouth.

BOBCAT LICKING TO REMOVE CHUNKS OF SNOW FROM BETWEEN ITS TOES. LEFT UN-ATTENDED, THE HARDENED SNOW COULD CAUSE SORES.

An animal's hide and scales, feathers, or fur provide its main protection from the elements. In the wild, a well-groomed animal is a healthy one.

Furbearers keep themselves clean and groomed by licking and by using their claws as combs. When fur gets wet it loses some of its insulating quality. Furry animals who swim always spend some time afterward on land rubbing their fur with their paws to help the air dry it out.

MUSKRAT RUBBING ITS FUR DRY AFTER SWIMMING

BEAVERS HAVE SPECIAL "COMBING CLAWS" ON THEIR HIND FEET. THEY USE THEM FOR GROOMING AND IN APPLYING OIL (MADE BY THEIR BODIES) TO KEEP THEIR FUR WATERPROOF

A BIRD'S FEATHERS OVERLAP ONE ANOTHER THE WAY SHINGLES DO ON A ROOF

ALL FEATHERS POINT DOWNWARD TO BEST SHED WIND AND WATER

A CHICKADEE ARRANGING ITS WING FEATHERS

Birds are forever fluffing and preening. Their feathers are arranged on their bodies to provide the best coverage and protection. Any feathers that are crooked, soiled, or stuck together must be groomed back into shape and position. In spring and fall birds molt, replacing hard-used feathers with fresh new ones. In most bird species this happens gradually, so they always have enough feathers for protection and flight. But ducks and geese cannot fly while they are molting. During this period they stay out on open water for safety.

NOTE: MOST BIRDS HAVE OIL GLANDS NEAR THE BASE OF THEIR TAILS. USING THEIR BEAKS, BIRDS SMEAR THE OIL OVER THEIR FEATHERS TO KEEP THEM SHINY AND CLEAN.

A MALLARD PREENING AND OILING ITS BREAST FEATHERS

A BEAVER SPLASHING ITS TAIL

Prey animals of the same species alert each other to the presence of danger by using quick signals. Rabbits thump their hind feet on the ground. Woodchucks whistle. Beavers smack their flat tails loudly on the water. Nervous deer stomp a foot once or twice. This warning vibrates through the ground for a considerable distance. Deer also snort before bolting.

White-tailed deer flash the white hair under their tails to signal a warning to other deer. As they run from danger their raised white tails act as "flags" that other deer can follow.

A DOE STOMPING HER RIGHT FRONT FOOT

THREE DOES WAVING THEIR TAIL FLAGS

BIG BUCKS BARELY SHOW THEIR FLAGS

When you are watching one animal and another suddenly appears on the scene, observe how each reacts to the presence of the other. Do they act friendly, indifferent, frightened, or hostile? If you see natural enemies confronting one another or even fighting, never interfere. Let what happens happen.

Different animals react differently to the sight of their natural enemies. Most flee. Some, however, react with rage. I once investigated the riotous sound of angry crows and found them circling and diving at a great horned owl that was roosting in a tree. The owl perched, blinking, as the screaming black birds tormented it. Then it leaned forward and pushed off from its limb, swooping low over the ground and away. The mob followed noisily.

After this, I learned that the great horned owl is the worst enemy crows have, attacking them at night when they are asleep and defenseless. The sight of an owl is like a living nightmare to crows. Whenever they discover an owl in the daylight, they mob it furiously to drive it away.

TWO RED-WINGED
BLACKBIRDS
ACKNOWLEDGING
ONE'S TERRITORIAL
BOUNDARY

Wild animals avoid fighting whenever possible. Even when pressed, they delay fighting as long as they can by posturing aggressively. This body language often ends a dispute nonviolently, with one animal frightening the other away.

HEAD BACK IN
SUBMISSION
TO A MORE
DOMINANT
BIRD

DEFENSIVE POSTURE
(MAY ATTACK)

NECK STRETCHED UP
SHOWS ALARM

HEAD PUMPING
SHOWS AGITATION

When defending themselves, birds fluff their feathers and hold their wings out. This puffed-up look not only says "keep your distance!," it makes them look larger and more formidable. Birds use posturing to express a wide range of emotions.

DROPPED WINGS
SHOWS AGGRESSION

A WING FLICK MAY
CHALLENGE ANOTHER'S
TERRITORY

A CANINE SURRENDER

When the growling, jaw-snapping, teeth-baring posturing of two canines fails to settle their argument, a fight ensues. There is always a winner—by death, flight, or surrender. All canines, wild or tame, surrender by rolling over and exposing their throat to their attacker. It is not a suicidal act. It is a move that effectively shuts off the winning animal's inclination to kill. Canines also use this posture when submitting to authority, as one wolf submits to the leader of the pack. I have two huge sled dogs. Each is bigger and stronger than I am. But when I pretend-fight with them, they eventually roll over and assume the surrender posture. They submit to my authority as their leader.

Some animals have a repertoire of ferocious-looking warnings but no real ability to back them up. Hognose snakes are not fighters, but they have an elaborate display of defensive postures. When first threatened, a hognose snake will coil and hiss like any other snake. If the danger continues, the snake pretends to be

A HOGNOSE SNAKE IS NAMED FOR ITS UP-TURNED SNOUT

HOGNOSE PLAYING
"COBRA"...

...AND PLAYING DEAD

ferocious. It spreads its neck like a cobra does.
It hisses more loudly and even strikes repeat-
edly, but it doesn't try to bite. If all that doesn't
work, the hognose snake, having used up all
its ferocity, finally flops over on its back and
hangs its tongue out like a bad actor playing a
death scene. Even if it is turned back over, the
silly snake will plop upside down again and re-
sume its act.

Most animals can back up their threats. Even
so, animals with powerful weapons use them
only when they must. Skunks are downright
stingy about using their potent weapon. They
go through a ritual of warning postures before
finally letting their molester have it, usually
right between the eyes.

When a skunk growls and pats its front
paws on the ground, it is giving its first warning. The second is two or three short hops
backward. Next, the skunk will lift its tail and
swing its body around, making sure that it can
see to take aim. This is the final warning!

THE LAST WARNING!

I once adopted a de-scented pet skunk named Grubs. Grubs taught me the important lesson that the best place to watch wild animals is in their natural habitat. He was a terrible house guest. Like all skunks, Grubs was nocturnal. He spent his days under a bedroom dresser. At night he came out to dig through

the trash for food scraps and hunt under the sink for crickets. Grubs tore a hole in the couch fabric and made a den inside amid the stuffings and springs. He'd unpot plants and spread the soil across the rug to search for insect larvae. Personally, Grubs was fastidious. He kept his fur groomed and glistening. He always used his litter pan and, to keep it clean, he kicked its contents out onto the floor. Grubs was instinctively wild. He would not let anyone touch him. When I tried to approach, he would go through all his skunk warnings. Then he'd swing around to shoot at me, even though his barrel was empty. I finally had to

take Grubs to a zoo where, happily, he was introduced to a lonely female skunk named, of all things, Petunia. That was ten years ago. Since skunks can live to be twelve years old, I figure Grubs and Petunia are now enjoying their sunset years together.

Everything we know about wildlife was discovered by watching. There is much more to learn. Keep a wildlife notebook and record what you see. Wherever you go there is wildlife to watch. Even in the largest cities, squirrels are sharing trees with bats, songbirds, and owls. There are pigeons nesting on ledges. Spiders design webs in windows and mice crisscross floors.

All kinds of animals, from mice to moose, have lived pieces of their lives with wildlife watchers nearby. I have shared some of my wildlife watching secrets with you. Now take them afield, use them, and find some secrets of your own. Then pass them along to a friend.